PLAN FOR PREPAREDNESS

BASIC PERSONAL AND FAMILY EMERGENCY PREPAREDNESS

KEITH PIPKIN

Contents

Foreword

So, why prepare?

No one is immune from disaster and it is important that we recognize the risks that we face everyday. Preparedness is not about surviving an apocalypse and rebuilding society. It is about the ability to get through whatever challenges may occur until conditions return to normal, whether that be for minutes, days or weeks. By implementing emergency preparedness we can improve our ability to respond, endure and recover from any emergency situation or disaster.

Preparedness is about being able to take care of ourselves and our family without relying on emergency services or others to come to our rescue. By being self-sufficient, we then become a resource to others and the community to help them through the shared struggle of a disaster event.

Being prepared means knowing what to do in response to an emergency situation, it is having supplies and skills to keep yourself and your family safe, healthy and thriving. It means having a plan.

That is why we prepare.

Introduction

There is no one-size-fits-all approach or universal plan for emergency preparedness. This book lays out a series of 10 recommended steps that should be evaluated, completed, adopted and practiced in a way that fits your situation.

This guide was written to accommodate a wide range of preparedness minded people. From an introduction to someone that is interested in emergency preparedness but has no idea what is needed or where to start, to someone that is seeking a refresher on fundamentals or wants to evaluate their current preparedness plans.

<u>What is Preparedness:</u>

Preparedness at its core is being ready, in advance, to deal with an emergency situation or disaster event.

The terms disaster or emergency broadly refer to a hazardous event resulting in danger or risk. This event threatens our personal safety, stability of society or way of life.

These hazards fall into one of the following categories:
1. Natural Hazard - An act of nature
2. Technological Hazard - Failures of systems and structures
3. Human Caused Hazard - Intentional actions of others meant to cause harm

Here are examples of each category:

Natural Hazards:
- Avalanche
- Drought
- Earthquake
- Epidemic / Pandemic
- Flood
- Hurricane
- Landslide
- Meteor or Asteroid Strike
- Solar Flare
- Tornado
- Tsunami
- Typhoon
- Volcano
- Wildfire
- Winter Storm

Technological Hazards:
- Chemical Emergency
- Dam Failure
- Financial Collapse
- Hazardous Release
- Home Fire
- Industrial Accident
- Multi-House Fire
- Nuclear Plant Release
- Pipeline Rupture
- Power Outage
- Train Derailment
- Utility Disruption

Human Caused Hazards:
- Active Shooter Incident
- Armed Assault
- Arson
- Attacks in Public Places
- Biological Attack
- Chemical Attack
- Cyber Attack
- EMP Attack
- Explosive Attack
- Nuclear Explosion
- Radiological Attack
- Terrorist Attack
- Water Contamination

STEP 1: Emergency Binder

Your Emergency Binder is the physical location of all written plans, important information / items and emergency reference materials assembled and put into a 3-ring binder. By having everything collected it becomes a single item that can be quickly referenced or taken when needed. I suggest either laminating or putting the pages in sheet protectors as well as larger items into binder zip pouches.

Given the importance and sensitivity of the contents, protection and security of your emergency binder is crucial. Your emergency binder needs to be stored in a location that is easily accessible, secure and protected from fire, water and theft.

The Emergency Binder consists of eight parts, which are listed below. Of those parts, the Family Emergency Plan is the most important to have but also the most difficult to create. The other parts consist of worksheets, checklists and exercises that will supplement and support the execution of your Family Emergency Plan.

Once completed, you will have all necessary information to prepare for and respond to any emergency situation.

Emergency Binder Contents:
1. Family Emergency Plan
2. Household Information
3. Communications Plan
4. Important Documents and Items
5. Getting Home Plan
6. Shelter-In-Home Actions
7. Evacuation / Bug Out Plan
8. Evacuation Checklist

Worksheets and templates throughout the book can be downloaded at www.planforpreparedness.com

1. Family Emergency Plan

The Family Emergency Plan is a written document based on the assessment of potential emergency situations or disaster events. Your plan should address all of the events most likely to occur because the response and actions may change. Everyone in the household should understand; what to do, where to go, and what skills and supplies will be needed.

Complete your Family Emergency Plan following the process outlined below. The worksheets, checklists and exercises throughout this book will assist and supplement your emergency plan and overall preparedness.

Once complete, assemble all of the items and put them into your Emergency Binder for organization.

Process For Creating Your Family Emergency Plan:

Hazard Assessment:

1. List all hazards or disaster events that could impact your family based on your location and their likelihood to occur. Consider disasters in your home, in your community, in your area, and nation-wide that may directly impact your household.

2. Give each hazard context such as; location, time of day, time of year, duration, magnitude and impact, based on a worst-case scenario outcome. The definition of worst-case is up to you to determine. Use your best guess or refer to similar events that have happened in the past. Think through this scenario as a sequence of events, considering the cascading effects that may result. There may also be several outcomes to evaluate.

   - For example: a January snowstorm drops 48" of snow in a 24-hour period. My vehicle gets stuck and I am unable to get help for 2 days given the weather conditions.

   - An alternate outcome would be: a January snowstorm drops 48" of snow in a 24-hour period. I am able to get home but unable to leave because the roads will not be cleared for 3 days. The power to my house goes out for 5 days.

3. Some hazards or disaster events may lead to a place where only the most extreme preparedness can keep you alive. This may be a direct nuclear strike on your home or a "doomsday" asteroid. Either way, these should be excluded from your analysis.

4. You should also exclude anything that seems very unlikely or beyond your personal ability to prepare for. This threshold is up to you. Some people believe an electromagnetic pulse (EMP) is likely, others do not.

What Are You Preparing For?

1. Now that you understand the potential hazards, it is time to narrow your focus on the event or events that will be basis of your preparedness efforts. You will find that by planning for one event, you may also be capable of handling other events, especially of lesser duration or impact. I suggest choosing multiple events, if the actions and preparations would be drastically different.

2. Starting small is just fine. You can focus on small scale disasters first and over time, grow your preparedness to handle the most severe situation you feel is likely.

Questions to consider:

- What disasters are most likely to affect our household?
- How will these disasters affect our household? For how long?
- Where will we most likely be? How does the time of day influence the event?
- How much warning will we have? How would we be warned or notified?

Plan Creation:

1. After defining the event or events you are preparing for, it is time to create an Emergency Plan that addresses each scenario. This may be one plan or several plans depending on the events. Think through what you would do at the beginning and throughout the duration of the event. This should be focused on major actions as a sequence of events. Broad items that are clear but nonspecific are sufficient to move forward through the plan. This may include items such as; get away from the area, contact emergency services, contact family, stay put, pick up kids, go home, get information about situation, gather items, prepare to leave, go to alternate location, and many more. This is the foundation of your emergency plan.

2. Complete the following sections of this guide and then return to your Emergency Plan. These items will help you better define the specifics of some of the major actions that could be taken.
   - Communications Plan (Page 26)
   - Getting Home Plan (Page 29)
   - Shelter-In-Home Actions (Page 31)
   - Evacuation / Bug out Plan (Page 32)
   - Evacuation Checklist (Page 42)

3. Next, fill in areas between the major actions and within the other plans by evaluating the basic requirements of; shelter, heat or cool, water, food, first-aid, security, etc. Your plan should address all of these throughout the duration of the event. This should primarily be focused on actions, not on supplies.

4. Then progress into less critical and more specific things like; transportation, clothing, communication, light, cooking, sleeping, hygiene, etc. Again, focus on actions, not supplies.

5. Finally, expand on any areas that need additional clarity or consider multiple options to handle a situation with specific details for each.

6. Complete your Emergency Plan and be proud. The effort and process of creating an emergency plan can be challenging but ultimately time well spent to keep yourself and your family safe, healthy and thriving through a disaster situation.

After going through a full analysis of hazards and disaster events you should have a good understanding of the risks of each. You should also have a clear impression of what actions, skills and supplies would be needed to properly prepare for and react to each scenario.

With a solid plan in place, the rest of this book will guide you through the emergency supplies that will help you during a disaster event. In a high-stress situation, you will have the peace of mind knowing; what to do, where to go, and what you need is available.

Questions to consider:

- What is our immediate action or response to the event?
- What should we do if the members of the household are not all together?
- Are smoke alarms and carbon monoxide detectors in place and in working condition?
- Where are the fire extinguishers? Do I know how to use a fire extinguisher?
- What are the escape routes from our home? From the second floor, first floor, basement?
- Do you know how to shut off the utilities to your home?
- Who should be contacted? How do we contact each other?
- What if cell phones are not working?
- Do I go home? How do I get home? What are alternate routes?
- How will your children or other family members get home?
- What if one or more person can't get home? What are alternate meeting locations?
- What are the next steps or additional actions that need to be taken?
- What events would require evacuation? When would we evacuate? Where would we go?
- If we have to leave home what would we take? Is it easy to collect and move?
- Where would I go if I need to bug out temporarily? What about permanently?
- Where are my important documents and are they in a safe and accessible location?
- Do I have what I need to shelter-in-place? For how long?
- Do I have sufficient supplies to get home? What if I am walking?
- Do I have the skills and supplies needed to last the duration of the event?
- How can we lessen the impact of the disaster on our household?

Testing Your Plan:

You should practice shelter-in-place and evacuation drills every 6 months. After each drill, the Family Emergency Plan should be reviewed and updated as needed.

Self Assessment:

As you are getting started with preparedness and repeated periodically, you should assess your current preparedness situation and identify anything that is unclear, incomplete or missing from your preparedness plan, skills and supplies.

Set goals to improve your situation. These goals should be specific and attainable with a clear date the goal is to be completed by. Start by laying out where you want your emergency preparedness to ultimately be. Break this down into small goals based on what you feel is the highest priority and most necessary. Through consistent small achievements you will be able to improve your preparedness over time and likely be more successful than setting a huge goal alone and then giving up before it is finished.

2. Household Information

Home Address

Home Address:	
Home Phone:	

Designated Emergency Meeting Locations

In Home:	
Outside of Home:	
Outside of Neighborhood:	
Outside of Town / City:	

Emergency Numbers

Emergency Service	Emergency Phone	Non Emergency Phone
Ambulance:	911	
Police:	911	
Fire:	911	
Poison Control:		
Other:		
Nearby Emergency Services:		
Hospital:	Phone:	
Address:		
Location (Major Crossroads):		
Hospital:	Phone:	
Address:		
Location (Major Crossroads):		
Urgent Care / ER:	Phone:	
Address:		
Location (Major Crossroads):		
Urgent Care / ER:	Phone:	
Address:		
Location (Major Crossroads):		
Fire Department:	Phone:	
Address:		
Location (Major Crossroads):		
Police:	Phone:	
Address:		
Location (Major Crossroads):		
County Sheriff:	Phone:	
Address:		
Location (Major Crossroads):		

Utility Providers

Electric:	
Account #:	Phone:
Login:	Password:
Gas:	
Account #:	Phone:
Login:	Password:
Water:	
Account #:	Phone:
Login:	Password:
Phone:	
Account #:	Phone:
Login:	Password:
Other:	
Account #:	Phone:
Login:	Password:

Other Services

Service	Emergency Phone	Non Emergency Phone
Animal Control:		
Veterinarian:		
Primary Doctor:		
Other:		

Home Information

HOA or Apartment:	
Emergency Phone:	Phone:
Contact:	
Email:	
Website:	
Login:	Password:
Insurance Company:	
Policy Number:	Claims Phone:
Agent:	Phone:
Website:	
Login:	Password:
Bank or Landlord:	
Account Number:	Phone:
Address:	
Email:	
Website:	
Login:	Password:

Home Layout / Diagram

In Home and Outside of Home meeting locations should also be shown on the Home Layout / Diagram

Home Layout / Diagram

Home Layout / Diagram

Nearby Emergency Services Map

Place a map of your home area with marked locations of nearby emergency services as listed previously below

☐ Home	☐ Urgent Care / ER
☐ Hospital	☐ Fire Department
☐ Hospital	☐ Police Department
☐ Urgent Care / ER	☐ County Sheriff

Place Your Map Here

Adult Family Member

Name:	
Date of Birth:	SSN:
Cell Phone:	Home Phone:
Email:	
Work Email:	Work Phone:
Employer:	Phone:
Address:	
Email:	
Work Contact Name:	Phone:
Email:	
Medical Information:	
Blood Type:	
Allergies:	
Medical Conditions:	
Medications:	
Medication Name:	Reason For Taking:
Dosage / Frequency:	
Prescribing Physician:	Prescription Date:
Pharmacy Phone:	Rx Number:
Medication Name:	Reason For Taking:
Dosage / Frequency:	
Prescribing Physician:	Prescription Date:
Pharmacy Phone:	Rx Number:
Medication Name:	Reason For Taking:
Dosage / Frequency:	
Prescribing Physician:	Prescription Date:
Pharmacy Phone:	Rx Number:
Primary Doctor:	
Organization:	Phone:
Address:	
Other Doctor:	Specialty:
Organization:	Phone:
Address:	
Other Doctor:	Specialty:
Organization:	Phone:
Address:	
Dentist:	
Organization:	Phone:
Address:	

Adult Family Member

Name:	
Date of Birth:	SSN:
Cell Phone:	Home Phone:
Email:	
Work Email:	Work Phone:
Employer:	Phone:
Address:	
Email:	
Work Contact Name:	Phone:
Email:	
Medical Information:	
Blood Type:	
Allergies:	
Medical Conditions:	
Medications:	
Medication Name:	Reason For Taking:
Dosage / Frequency:	
Prescribing Physician:	Prescription Date:
Pharmacy Phone:	Rx Number:
Medication Name:	Reason For Taking:
Dosage / Frequency:	
Prescribing Physician:	Prescription Date:
Pharmacy Phone:	Rx Number:
Medication Name:	Reason For Taking:
Dosage / Frequency:	
Prescribing Physician:	Prescription Date:
Pharmacy Phone:	Rx Number:
Primary Doctor:	
Organization:	Phone:
Address:	
Other Doctor:	Specialty:
Organization:	Phone:
Address:	
Other Doctor:	Specialty:
Organization:	Phone:
Address:	
Dentist:	
Organization:	Phone:
Address:	

Teen Family Member

Name:	
Date of Birth:	SSN:
Cell Phone:	Alt. Phone:
Email:	Alt. Email:
Employer:	Phone:
Address:	
Email:	
Work Contact Name:	Phone:
Email:	
School:	Phone:
Address:	
Email:	
School Contact Name:	Phone:
Email:	
Medical Information:	
Blood Type:	
Allergies:	
Medical Conditions:	
Medications:	
Medication Name:	Reason For Taking:
Dosage / Frequency:	
Prescribing Physician:	Prescription Date:
Pharmacy Phone:	Rx Number:
Medication Name:	Reason For Taking:
Dosage / Frequency:	
Prescribing Physician:	Prescription Date:
Pharmacy Phone:	Rx Number:
Medication Name:	Reason For Taking:
Dosage / Frequency:	
Prescribing Physician:	Prescription Date:
Pharmacy Phone:	Rx Number:
Primary Doctor:	
Organization:	Phone:
Address:	
Other Doctor:	Specialty:
Organization:	Phone:
Address:	
Dentist:	
Organization:	Phone:
Address:	

Teen Family Member

Name:	
Date of Birth:	SSN:
Cell Phone:	Alt. Phone:
Email:	Alt. Email:
Employer:	Phone:
Address:	
Email:	
Work Contact Name:	Phone:
Email:	
School:	Phone:
Address:	
Email:	
School Contact Name:	Phone:
Email:	
Medical Information:	
Blood Type:	
Allergies:	
Medical Conditions:	
Medications:	
Medication Name:	Reason For Taking:
Dosage / Frequency:	
Prescribing Physician:	Prescription Date:
Pharmacy Phone:	Rx Number:
Medication Name:	Reason For Taking:
Dosage / Frequency:	
Prescribing Physician:	Prescription Date:
Pharmacy Phone:	Rx Number:
Medication Name:	Reason For Taking:
Dosage / Frequency:	
Prescribing Physician:	Prescription Date:
Pharmacy Phone:	Rx Number:
Primary Doctor:	
Organization:	Phone:
Address:	
Other Doctor:	Specialty:
Organization:	Phone:
Address:	
Dentist:	
Organization:	Phone:
Address:	

Child Family Member

Name:	
Date of Birth:	SSN:
Cell Phone:	Alt. Phone:
Email:	Alt. Email:
School:	Phone:
Address:	
Email:	
Teacher:	Phone:
Email:	
Other Caregiver:	Phone:
Address:	
Email:	
Contact Name:	Phone:
Email:	
Medical Information:	
Blood Type:	
Allergies:	
Medical Conditions:	
Medications:	
Medication Name:	Reason For Taking:
Dosage / Frequency:	
Prescribing Physician:	Prescription Date:
Pharmacy Phone:	Rx Number:
Medication Name:	Reason For Taking:
Dosage / Frequency:	
Prescribing Physician:	Prescription Date:
Pharmacy Phone:	Rx Number:
Medication Name:	Reason For Taking:
Dosage / Frequency:	
Prescribing Physician:	Prescription Date:
Pharmacy Phone:	Rx Number:
Primary Doctor:	
Organization:	Phone:
Address:	
Other Doctor:	Specialty:
Organization:	Phone:
Address:	
Dentist:	
Organization:	Phone:
Address:	

Child Family Member

Name:	
Date of Birth:	SSN:
Cell Phone:	Alt. Phone:
Email:	Alt. Email:
School:	Phone:
Address:	
Email:	
Teacher:	Phone:
Email:	
Other Caregiver:	Phone:
Address:	
Email:	
Contact Name:	Phone:
Email:	
Medical Information:	
Blood Type:	
Allergies:	
Medical Conditions:	
Medications:	
Medication Name:	Reason For Taking:
Dosage / Frequency:	
Prescribing Physician:	Prescription Date:
Pharmacy Phone:	Rx Number:
Medication Name:	Reason For Taking:
Dosage / Frequency:	
Prescribing Physician:	Prescription Date:
Pharmacy Phone:	Rx Number:
Medication Name:	Reason For Taking:
Dosage / Frequency:	
Prescribing Physician:	Prescription Date:
Pharmacy Phone:	Rx Number:
Primary Doctor:	
Organization:	Phone:
Address:	
Other Doctor:	Specialty:
Organization:	Phone:
Address:	
Dentist:	
Organization:	Phone:
Address:	

Additional Contacts: Family, Friends and Neighbors

Name:		Description:
Address:		
Cell Phone:	Home Phone:	Work Phone:
Email:		
Name:		Description:
Address:		
Cell Phone:	Home Phone:	Work Phone:
Email:		
Name:		Description:
Address:		
Cell Phone:	Home Phone:	Work Phone:
Email:		
Name:		Description:
Address:		
Cell Phone:	Home Phone:	Work Phone:
Email:		
Name:		Description:
Address:		
Cell Phone:	Home Phone:	Work Phone:
Email:		

Additional Contacts: Out-of-Area Contacts

Name:		Description:
Address:		
Cell Phone:	Home Phone:	Work Phone:
Email:		
Name:		Description:
Address:		
Cell Phone:	Home Phone:	Work Phone:
Email:		
Name:		Description:
Address:		
Cell Phone:	Home Phone:	Work Phone:
Email:		
Name:		Description:
Address:		
Cell Phone:	Home Phone:	Work Phone:
Email:		

Vehicle Information

Year:		Make:		Model:	
Color:		VIN:			
License Plate:		Description:			
Insurance Company:					
Policy Number:					
Agent:				Phone:	
Claims Phone:					

Year:		Make:		Model:	
Color:		VIN:			
License Plate:		Description:			
Insurance Company:					
Policy Number:					
Agent:				Phone:	
Claims Phone:					

Year:		Make:		Model:	
Color:		VIN:			
License Plate:		Description:			
Insurance Company:					
Policy Number:					
Agent:				Phone:	
Claims Phone:					

Year:		Make:		Model:	
Color:		VIN:			
License Plate:		Description:			
Insurance Company:					
Policy Number:					
Agent:				Phone:	
Claims Phone:					

Year:		Make:		Model:	
Color:		VIN:			
License Plate:		Description:			
Insurance Company:					
Policy Number:					
Agent:				Phone:	
Claims Phone:					

Financial Information

Account Name:	Account Type:
Institution:	Account Number:
Address:	
Website:	Phone:
Login:	Password:
Account Name:	Account Type:
Institution:	Account Number:
Address:	
Website:	Phone:
Login:	Password:
Account Name:	Account Type:
Institution:	Account Number:
Address:	
Website:	Phone:
Login:	Password:
Account Name:	Account Type:
Institution:	Account Number:
Address:	
Website:	Phone:
Login:	Password:
Account Name:	Account Type:
Institution:	Account Number:
Address:	
Website:	Phone:
Login:	Password:
Account Name:	Account Type:
Institution:	Account Number:
Address:	
Website:	Phone:
Login:	Password:
Account Name:	Account Type:
Institution:	Account Number:
Address:	
Website:	Phone:
Login:	Password:
Account Name:	Account Type:
Institution:	Account Number:
Address:	
Website:	Phone:
Login:	Password:

Important Access, Websites and Passwords

This area is broad and meant to capture any important information that was previously not covered.

This could include: devices, computer or phone, login or passwords; email account passwords; codes or combinations to safes, locks, doors, gates, garages; personal accounts and services; or any other item that may be important for others to access.

Description:	Description:
Website:	Website:
Login:	Login:
Password:	Password:
Description:	Description:
Website:	Website:
Login:	Login:
Password:	Password:
Description:	Description:
Website:	Website:
Login:	Login:
Password:	Password:
Description:	Description:
Login:	Login:
Password:	Password:
Description:	Description:
Login:	Login:
Password:	Password:
Description:	Description:
Login:	Login:
Password:	Password:
Description:	Description:
Code / Combination:	Code / Combination:
Description:	Description:
Code / Combination:	Code / Combination:
Description:	Description:
Code / Combination:	Code / Combination:
Description:	Description:
Description:	Description:
Description:	Description:

3. Communications Plan

A communications plan is essential to your Family Emergency Plan. It establishes a mutually understood, effective and simple system for contacting one another in an emergency situation.

An effective method for building a communications plan is to use the PACE method. PACE stands for Primary, Alternate, Contingency and Emergency. This allows for several alternative ways of communicating should one or more fail to work. These are arranged with the best and easiest methods first and the least effective and most difficult methods last.

Primary - Is the first mode of communication using a common, simple and effective method. Continuously monitored and available under normal conditions.

For example: call via cell phone or group text message

Alternate - Uses another common mode of communication but one that is not as simple or effective. Often used or monitored in addition to the primary method.

For example: call via land line phone, text message, social media message, or messenger

Contingency - Less effective and more difficult than the previous methods. This could include a means that is not continuously monitored or easily accessible.

For example: email, or Ham radio via a repeater

Emergency - The method of last resort. Is used when all other methods fail. It could have significant delays in communications. Typically not monitored until other methods have failed.

For example: FRS / GMRS or Ham radio, or sending written messages

Depending on the size of your household or group, it may also be useful to establish a phone tree or some form of structure to make contact and pass information. Just be sure to establish the procedures to follow if someone cannot be reached and how to provide confirmation that the message was received by everyone.

Primary Method of Communications:

Details:

When to Make First Contact:

When to Make Regular Contact:

If Unable to Reach / No Response:

When to Use Alternate Method:

Alternate Method of Communications:

Details:

When to Make First Contact:

When to Make Regular Contact:

If Unable to Reach / No Response:

When to Use Contingency Method:

Contingency Method of Communications:

Details:

When to Make First Contact:

When to Make Regular Contact:

If Unable to Reach / No Response:

When to Use Emergency Method:

Emergency Method of Communications:

Details:

When to Make First Contact:

When to Make Regular Contact:

If Unable to Reach / No Response:

If Contact Is Not Made After Trying All Methods:

Notes:

4. Important Documents and Items

In addition to your Family Emergency Plan and Household Information it is important to gather documents and items that cannot be easily replaced or would be important to have in the event that your home is destroyed or you cannot return to your home.

These can be original documents, copies or digital copies placed on a thumb drive.

These items need to be stored in a location that is easily accessible, secure and protected from fire, water and theft. They also need to be quickly accessible when needed and taken with you if you have to evacuate.

Personal and Vital Documents:
- ☐ Driver's License
- ☐ Social Security Card
- ☐ Birth / Death Certificate
- ☐ Passport
- ☐ Marriage License
- ☐ Military Discharge Papers
- ☐ Will
- ☐ Powers of Attorney
- ☐ Trust Documents
- ☐ Firearm Serial Numbers
- ☐ Safe Deposit and Safe Keys and Combos
- ☐ Credit Cards
- ☐ Adoption / Foster Records
- ☐ Naturalization / Immigration Documents
- ☐ School Records
- ☐ Educational Degrees

Financial Documents:
- ☐ Savings Bonds, CD, Stocks and Bonds
- ☐ Real Estate Deeds
- ☐ Mortgage Documents
- ☐ Property Tax Records
- ☐ Inventory of Assets
- ☐ Vehicle Titles
- ☐ Income Tax Returns
- ☐ Rental / Lease Agreements
- ☐ Loan Documents

Medical and Health Documents:
- ☐ Medical Records
- ☐ Immunization Records
- ☐ Prescriptions
- ☐ Insurance Cards
- ☐ Advanced Care Directives

Other Important Items
- ☐ Keys: Vehicles, House, etc.
- ☐ Photos
- ☐ Cash (Small Bills)
- ☐ Maps of Surrounding Areas
- ☐ Maps of Evacuation Route
- ☐ Pet Vet Records

5. Getting Home Plan

The getting home plan is used to assess how you would get home in the event of an emergency. The route and means of getting home may vary greatly based upon the specific disaster scenario. For example: a severe storm may allow for typical routes to be taken or road closures and accidents may require that alternate routes be used.

Additionally, events like tornadoes, hurricanes or flooding may restrict or prevent getting home. In that scenario, a location outside of your neighborhood or even outside of your city/town should be established as an alternative meeting location. An ideal meeting location would be your bug out location which is addressed further in Section 7, "From Work to Bug Out Location" (See Page 38).

For the most simplistic scenario and basic getting home plan we will assume you can get home but may have to take alternative routes and/or alternative means of transportation.

This exercise should be done for each member of the household following the same steps for each person.

Thing to consider and address beyond the basic getting home plan:
1. How does this plan vary on non-working or non-school days?
2. How many possible starting locations should be considered? What if you are across town or out of town?
3. How does this plan vary for people who do not have a fixed work location?
4. What are alternate modes of transportation available?
5. Who and how will you pick up children or other members of the family who cannot get themselves home?

Location:	
Address:	
Typical Days and Hours at Location:	
Typical Mode of Transportation:	
Primary Route:	
Distance to Travel:	Time to Travel:
Alternate Route 1:	
Distance to Travel:	Time to Travel:
Alternate Route 2:	
Distance to Travel:	Time to Travel:
Alternate Modes of Transportation:	
Notes:	

Getting Home Map

Place a map of your get home route with marked locations of stops and resources below

☐ Work	☐ Food	☐ Rest Stop	☐ _____
☐ Home	☐ Medical	☐ Overnight	☐ _____
☐ Water	☐ Supplies	☐ Meeting Spot	☐ _____
☐ Fuel	☐ Cache	☐ Hazard	☐ _____

Place Your Map Here

6. Shelter-In-Home Actions

In the event of a disaster, you will most likely want to get home and stay home unless you are unable to get home or absolutely have to evacuate. Some steps need to be taken right away as well as steps that can be taken to monitor and assess the extent of the situation. There are other steps that would need to be taken specific to the disaster event.

Below is a list of shelter-in-home actions that should be considered or taken, depending on the situation. This list should be adapted and modified for your unique situation and specific needs of your family. This should also be incorporated and practiced as part of your Family Emergency Plan.

Prior to a Disaster Event:
☐ Set up disaster warning alerts, including: phone app notifications, text messages and email
☐ Establish a designated shelter room (preferably an interior room or basement)
☐ Build a 72-Hour Kit

Additional Precautions:
☐ Precut plastic sheeting to fit over external doors and windows
☐ Precut plywood sheets for protecting windows

After a Disaster Event:
☐ Remain Calm
☐ Bring your family and pets inside
☐ Lock all doors and windows
☐ Monitor news: TV, Internet, social media, AM/FM radio, weather radio, Ham radio, etc. for information and instructions
☐ Contact any household members that are not home as well as additional family, friends and preparedness group / network
☐ Retrieve your disaster supplies and take them to your shelter room

Power Outage
☐ Monitor AM/FM radio, weather radio or Ham radio
☐ Keep the refrigerator and freezer closed. Food will keep cold for about 4 hours in the refrigerator and about 48 hours in a freezer
☐ Using alternate cooling, heating and cooking sources. Do not use gas stove or oven for heating, always use grills, camp stoves, camp lanterns and generators outdoors
☐ Ensure emergency light sources are accessible

Pandemic, Chemical, Biological, Nuclear/Radiological Disaster
☐ Install HEPA furnace filters to filter out contaminants (Biological)
☐ Turn off HVAC system, close windows and external vents
☐ Once inside, wash yourself with soap and water and put on clean clothes
☐ Seal windows and doors with plastic sheeting and duct tape
☐ Wash hands with soap and water frequently
☐ Cover mouth and nose with filter face mask or multi-layer fabric
☐ Stay indoors until advised it is safe to leave
☐ Avoid other people

This list is valuable but not comprehensive. For every disaster situation, additional or alternate steps needs to be taken based on the event specifics, severity and your specific home construction and location. There are numerous additional resources on the topic that should be referenced and followed.

7. Evacuation / Bug Out Plan

In the event of a disaster situation there may reach a point where you are either required or need to leave your home for an undetermined amount of time which could be indefinite. It is important to plan out in advance exactly where you would go and what you would take. An evacuation or bug out plan follows the same path of logic as the "Getting Home Plan" but with the starting point being your home and the end destination being your bug out location. As with any other emergency plan, it is important to establish several alternate bug out locations and intermediate or stopping points on the way to your bug out location.

The process of evaluating and selecting a bug out location can be challenging and is beyond the scope of this book. The bottom line is that you need to establish predetermined bug out locations.

Your bug out plan should be repeatedly practiced and refined using various modes of transportation including on foot.

In addition to filling out the below tables, you should create maps showing each bug out location, primary and alternate routes, stop and overnight locations as well as fuel, food, water and other resources or significant item along the route.

Primary Bug Out Location:

Location:	GPS Coordinates:
Address:	
Primary Mode of Transportation:	
Primary Route:	
Distance to Travel:	Time to Travel:
Alternate Route 1:	
Distance to Travel:	Time to Travel:
Alternate Route 2:	
Distance to Travel:	Time to Travel:
Alternate Modes of Transportation:	
Notes:	

Bug Out Map - Primary Location

Place a map of your bug out route with marked locations of stops and resources below

- ☐ Home
- ☐ Bug Out Location
- ☐ Water
- ☐ Fuel

- ☐ Food
- ☐ Medical
- ☐ Supplies
- ☐ Cache

- ☐ Rest Stop
- ☐ Overnight
- ☐ Meeting Spot
- ☐ Hazard

- ☐ _____
- ☐ _____
- ☐ _____
- ☐ _____

Place Your Map Here

Alternate Bug Out Location 1:

Location:	GPS Coordinates:
Address:	
Primary Mode of Transportation:	

Primary Route:

Distance to Travel:	Time to Travel:

Alternate Route 1:

Distance to Travel:	Time to Travel:

Alternate Route 2:

Distance to Travel:	Time to Travel:

Alternate Modes of Transportation:

Notes:

Bug Out Map - Alternate Location 1

Place a map of your bug out route with marked locations of stops and resources below

- Home
- Bug Out Location
- Water
- Fuel

- Food
- Medical
- Supplies
- Cache

- Rest Stop
- Overnight
- Meeting Spot
- Hazard

Place Your Map Here

Alternate Bug Out Location 2:

Location:	GPS Coordinates:
Address:	
Primary Mode of Transportation:	

Primary Route:

Distance to Travel:	Time to Travel:

Alternate Route 1:

Distance to Travel:	Time to Travel:

Alternate Route 2:

Distance to Travel:	Time to Travel:

Alternate Modes of Transportation:

Notes:

Bug Out Map - Alternate Location 2

Place a map of your bug out route with marked locations of stops and resources below

☐ Home	☐ Food	☐ Rest Stop	☐
☐ Bug Out Location	☐ Medical	☐ Overnight	☐
☐ Water	☐ Supplies	☐ Meeting Spot	☐
☐ Fuel	☐ Cache	☐ Hazard	☐

Place Your Map Here

From Work to Bug Out Location:

An alternate route to plan, as discussed in Section 5 "Getting Home Plan" (See Page 29), is the scenario where you are at work but cannot go home for any reason requiring an alternate meeting location. Your bug out location should serve as a known and established destination.

Work Location:	
Address:	
Bug Out Location:	GPS Coordinates:
Address:	
Primary Mode of Transportation:	
Primary Route:	
Distance to Travel:	Time to Travel:
Alternate Route 1:	
Distance to Travel:	Time to Travel:
Alternate Route 2:	
Distance to Travel:	Time to Travel:
Alternate Modes of Transportation:	
Notes:	

From Work to Bug Out Location Map

Place a map of your route from work to your bug out location with marked locations of stops and resources below

☐ Home	☐ Food	☐ Rest Stop	☐
☐ Bug Out Location	☐ Medical	☐ Overnight	☐
☐ Water	☐ Supplies	☐ Meeting Spot	☐
☐ Fuel	☐ Cache	☐ Hazard	☐

Place Your Map Here

From Work to Bug Out Location:

Work Location:	
Address:	
Bug Out Location:	GPS Coordinates:
Address:	
Primary Mode of Transportation:	

Primary Route:

Distance to Travel:	Time to Travel:

Alternate Route 1:

Distance to Travel:	Time to Travel:

Alternate Route 2:

Distance to Travel:	Time to Travel:

Alternate Modes of Transportation:

Notes:

From Work to Bug Out Location Map

Place a map of your route from work to your bug out location with marked locations of stops and resources below

Home	Food	Rest Stop	
Bug Out Location	Medical	Overnight	
Water	Supplies	Meeting Spot	
Fuel	Cache	Hazard	

Place Your Map Here

8. Evacuation Checklist

In the event that you must leave your home, an evacuation checklist should be followed to guide you through the actions to take prior to leaving. By having a checklist, it will serve as a simple reference tool to be used during what is likely to be a stressful situation. The below list covers basic items and broad categories. Additional effort should be taken to create a detailed checklist that includes item details and locations. You should also assess your method of transportation which will most likely be your vehicle for the available space. You need to ensure that what you intend on taking will fit.

Depending on the situation and amount of time you have to assemble and load these items, will determine if only the essentials can be taken or if additional items can be included.

The items on this list should be located together, organized, labeled, and in containers or bags that are easily transported. Having items dispersed throughout your home or sitting unpacked (such as a shelf full of items) will cause the process to take considerably more time and effort.

Do Before Leaving and Take With You:

- ☐ Important Documents and Items
- ☐ 72-Hour Kit
- ☐ Bug Out /Get Home Bag
- ☐ Car Kit (if not already in car)
- ☐ Wear sturdy shoes
- ☐ Purse / Wallet, cell phone, keys
- ☐ Prescription medications
- ☐ Leave marking or note of where you are going and contact information
- ☐ Lock the house
- ☐ Lock any remaining vehicles
- ☐ Phone Charger
- ☐ Any special needs items
    - ☐ _____
    - ☐ _____
    - ☐ _____
    - ☐ _____
    - ☐ _____
- ☐ Infant Items
- ☐ Pet Items
    - ☐ Food
    - ☐ Medicines
    - ☐ Leash
    - ☐ Carrier

- ☐ Additional food and water
- ☐ Additional firearms and ammo
- ☐ Additional preparedness equipment
- ☐ Additional tools and supplies
- ☐ _____
- ☐ _____
- ☐ _____
- ☐ _____
- ☐ _____
- ☐ _____
- ☐ _____
- ☐ _____
- ☐ _____
- ☐ _____
- ☐ _____
- ☐ Other / Optional:
    - ☐ Turn off the power to the house, main breaker
    - ☐ Turn off the water to the house, main water line
    - ☐ Turn off the gas to the house, at gas meter
    - ☐ _____
    - ☐ _____
    - ☐ _____

Evacuation Note / Leave Behind Note

When you evacuate your home or abandon your vehicle, you should leave a way for others to find you. This could be a paper note on the front door or garage door or something more visible and permanent, such as using a permanent marker or spray paint. Be sure to leave information of when you left, where you are going and how you can be contacted.

In some cases, you may not want to leave the address of where you are going. If so, use a term or reference that can be understood by someone that knows you but would not be understood by others and includes the date that you left. For example: "Went to Joe's parents' house on 2/19" or "Went to the cabin on 3/1".

Attention:

Due to an emergency situation,
☐ I have abandoned my vehicle
☐ I have evacuated my home

Date: _____   Time: _____
Name: _____
Phone Number: _____
Address: _____

My travel plans and emergency contact information are below. Please confirm my safe arrival before discarding this note.

Travel Plans: _____
_____
_____
_____

Emergency Contact Information:

Name: _____
Phone Number: _____
Address: _____

STEP 2: First Aid Kit

Every household should have a first aid kit to treat minor injuries. Additionally, everyone should have an Individual First Aid Kit (IFAK) if they are in a situation or area where medical assistance is not readily available. Throughout this guide, most every list will include a first aid kit. First aid is a fundamental part of emergency preparedness.

Having first aid supplies is not a substitute for having first aid skills. Everyone should have basic first aid and CPR training. Additional training, such as treating major injuries is a significant bonus to your family's overall health if emergency response is not available.

In addition to a first aid kit, you should also know your blood-type. In the event that you need to give or get blood, this is good to know. I have my blood-type marked on my IFAK so an emergency responder has this information if I am unable to provide it to them.

Blood-Type Compatibility Chart:

Blood-Type	Donates Blood To:	Receives Blood From:
A+	A+, AB+	A+, A-, O+, O-
A-	A+, A-, AB+, AB-	A-, O-
B+	B+, AB+	B+, B-, O+, O-
B-	B+, B-, AB+, AB-	B-, O-
AB+	AB+	Everyone
AB-	AB+, AB-	AB-, A-, B-, O-
O+	O+, A+, B+, AB+	O+, O-
O-	Everyone	O-

The following are lists of several first aid kits from basic to family. Each serves a purpose in your overall preparedness supplies.

LEVEL 0: Everyday Carry (EDC) First Aid Kit

Basic first aid supplies that can fit in a purse or small pouch. These items are useful for minor cuts and scrapes but will not address any major wounds. This kit is not intended to replace an Individual First Aid Kit (IFAK) but instead used for portability and situations where medical help is available if needed.

- ☐ (1) Pouch or bag, to hold kit contents
- ☐ (1) Pair Large Nitrile Gloves
- ☐ (1) Celox / Quikclot 2g powder or 25g sponge or gauze 3" x 24" (stops bleeding)
- ☐ (1) Pack Steri-Strips (5 strips) (butterfly closure)
- ☐ (4) Alcohol wipes
- ☐ (5) 1" x 3" Adhesive bandages
- ☐ (3) 2" x 3" Adhesive bandages
- ☐ (10) Non-sterile 4" x 4" gauzes
- ☐ (5) Non-Stick sterile dressing 2" x 3" or 3" x 4"
- ☐ (1) Cloth Medical Tape or Transpore surgical tape or duct tape 1" x 10 yards

LEVEL 1: IFAK (Individual First Aid Kit)

Every member of the family or group should carry a lightweight mobile kit called an IFAK. It allows for treatment of some common medical problems that may be encountered and to stop bleeding for serious problems until medical help is found.

- ☐ (1) Pouch or bag, to hold kit contents
- ☐ (2) Pairs Large Nitrile Gloves
- ☐ (1) Celox / Quikclot 2g powder or 25g sponge or gauze 3" x 24" (stops bleeding)
- ☐ (1) 6" Israeli bandage or other compression bandage
- ☐ (1) Triangular Bandage with safety pins or Bandana (sling)
- ☐ (1) Pack Steri-Strips (5 strips) (butterfly closure)
- ☐ (1) Super glue or medical glue packet (wound closure)
- ☐ (10) Alcohol wipes
- ☐ (2) Packets burn gel
- ☐ (2) Triple antibiotic ointment (Neosporin or Bacitracin)
- ☐ (2) Benzalkonium (BZK) anti-microbial / antiseptic wipes
- ☐ (1) Hand sanitizer
- ☐ (5) 1" x 3" Adhesive bandages
- ☐ (5) 2" x 3" Adhesive bandages
- ☐ (1) Sheet Moleskin blister bandage
- ☐ (2) Sterile ABD dressing 5" x 9" (abdominal pads)
- ☐ (10) Non-sterile 4" x 4" gauzes (or 3" x 3")
- ☐ (5) Sterile 4" x 4" gauzes (or 3" x 3")
- ☐ (5) Non-Stick sterile dressing 2" x 3" or 3" x 4"
- ☐ (1) Roller gauze sterile dressing
- ☐ (1) Cloth Medical Tape or Transpore surgical tape 1" x 10 yards
- ☐ (1) Sharpie permanent marker
- ☐ (1) Lip Balm (Chapstick, etc.)
- ☐ (2) Zip Lock bags quart size

LEVEL 1.5: Advanced IFAK

The Advanced IFAK includes all of the items from the Level 1 IFAK and adds several items typically found in commercial or military kits, most importantly a tourniquet to treat more severe situations.

- ☐ All items from the Level 1 Kit
- ☐ (1) CAT or SOFT-T Tourniquet
- ☐ (1) Stainless steel bandage scissors 5.5" or 7.25"
- ☐ (1) HALO Chest Seal
- ☐ (1) Nasopharyngeal Airway (opens blocked airway)
- ☐ (1) Duct tape 2" x 50"
- ☐ (1) 4" or 3" ACE Wrap

LEVEL 2: Family First Aid Kit

Designed for a single family, this is the minimum amount of basic first aid equipment to handle common household emergencies that may be encountered in any situation.

Quantities should be adjusted based on the number of people in your family or group.

- ☐ (1) Backpack or medium bag, to hold kit contents
- ☐ (1) First aid reference book
- ☐ (5) Pairs Large Nitrile Gloves
- ☐ (1) CAT Tourniquet
- ☐ (1) LED headlamp or penlight
- ☐ (1) Sharpie permanent marker
- ☐ (2) Zip Lock bags quart size
- ☐ (1) Lip Balm (Chapstick, etc.)
- ☐ (1) Duct tape 2" x 50"
- ☐ (4) Dust / Filtration Face Mask (Surgical and 3M N100)
- ☐ (1) Thermometer
- ☐ (1) Eye Wash Solution 16oz
- ☐ (2) Eye pads
- ☐ (1) Cold pack / Hot pack
- ☐ (10) Water purification tablets (Katadyn, Micropur or Potable Aqua)
- ☐ (1) SAM Splint 36"
- ☐ (1) Stainless steel bandage scissors 7.25"
- ☐ (1) Tweezers
- ☐ (1) Nail Scissors
- ☐ (1) Straight hemostat clamp 5"
- ☐ (1) Nasopharyngeal Airway (opens blocked airway)
- ☐ (1) Celox / Quikclot 2g powder or 25g sponge or gauze 3" x 24" (stops bleeding)
- ☐ (1) 6" Israeli bandage or other compression bandage
- ☐ (1) Triangular Bandage with safety pins or Bandana (sling)
- ☐ (1) 4" ACE Wrap
- ☐ (1) 2-0 Nylon suture
- ☐ (1) Pack Steri-Strips (5 strips) (butterfly closure)
- ☐ (1) Super glue or medical glue packet (wound closure)
- ☐ (10) Alcohol wipes
- ☐ (2) Packets burn gel
- ☐ (2) Triple antibiotic ointment (Neosporin or Bacitracin)
- ☐ (6) Benzalkonium (BZK) anti-microbial / antiseptic wipes
- ☐ (10) Povidone-iodine (PVP / Betadine) wipes
- ☐ (1) Hand sanitizer

☐ (20) 1" x 3" Adhesive bandages
☐ (10) 2" x 3" Adhesive bandages
☐ (1) Sheet Moleskin blister bandage
☐ (2) Sterile ABD dressing 5" x 9" (abdominal pads)
☐ (20) Non-sterile 4" x 4" gauzes (or 3" x 3")
☐ (10) Sterile 4" x 4" gauzes (or 3" x 3")
☐ (5) Non-Stick sterile dressing 2" x 3" or 3" x 4"
☐ (1) Roller gauze sterile dressing
☐ (1) Cloth Medical Tape or Transpore surgical tape 1" x 10 yards
☐ (1) Pain Relief - Acetaminophen (Tylenol) / Ibuprofen (Advil)/ Aspirin
☐ (1) 1% Hydrocortisone Cream
☐ (1) Allergy Relief - Benadryl (Diphenhydramine) / Claritin (Loratadine)
☐ (1) Imodium (Loperamide)
☐ (1) Pepto-Bismol (Bismuth Subsalicylate) or Antacid
☐ (1) Laxative
☐ (1) Sunblock
☐ (1) Insect Repellant
☐ (1) Gold bond foot powder
☐ (10) Tampons
☐ (1) Commercial Dental Kit

Other Items to Include:
☐ Epi Pen (Epinephrine)
☐ Prescription Medications
☐ Antibiotics
☐ Antacids
☐ 2.5% Lidocane cream (local anesthetic)
☐ Hydrogen Peroxide or Rubbing Alcohol
☐ Bactine Spray (antiseptic and pain reliever)

STEP 3: Everyday Carry

The purpose of everyday carry is to ensure that you have some basic items with you at all times. You will not always have the ability to carry or even be near your Bug Out Bag or vehicle. By having essentials on you, may become your only resource.

What you choose for your everyday carry should be adjusted to your personal situation and preferences. Your job may limit your ability to wear and/or have certain items. If that is the case, it is a good idea to have at least a change of shoes and ideally a change of clothes with you at work.

If your job permits, listed are some recommended clothing and items to have or wear everyday:

Items Worn:
- ☐ Sturdy waterproof shoes / boots
- ☐ Non-cotton socks
- ☐ Heavy duty belt (Riggers belt)
- ☐ Tactical pants (5.11 Tactical)
- ☐ Watch
- ☐ Sunglasses

Carried in Pockets/On Belt:
- ☐ Wallet
- ☐ Cell phone
- ☐ Handgun, pepper spray or taser
- ☐ Handgun holster
- ☐ Spare magazine(s)
- ☐ Small flashlight
- ☐ Folding pocket knife
- ☐ Multi-tool
- ☐ Emergency cash (small bills)
- ☐ BIC Lighter
- ☐ Pen and Notepad
- ☐ Tourniquet

Additional Items - Pouch Carried:
- ☐ Pouch to hold contents
- ☐ Small first aid kit (Level 0)
- ☐ Key chain multipurpose tool
- ☐ Matches, butane lighter or other fire starter
- ☐ EMT shears
- ☐ Paracord
- ☐ Sharpie permanent marker
- ☐ Flashlight batteries
- ☐ Additional ammunition
- ☐ Pocket survival kit

STEP 4: Bug Out / Get Home Bag

A Bug Out Bag (BOB) or Get Home Bag is a packed and ready bag that contains supplies and equipment needed in the event that you either need to evacuate your home to get to another location (bug out) or need to get home following a disaster event. The BOB is meant to be portable and sustain you for a limited amount of time until you reach your destination.

Every member of your family or group needs their own BOB and while some items can be shared, it is important that each BOB is capable of sustaining the user independently in the event that one BOB is left or lost or a member of the group gets separated.

There are numerous variables to consider when assembling a BOB. The most important being the intended length of use. Depending on the distance you may need to travel, the overall contents should be adjusted while maintaining a weight that is manageable to carry on foot. Target 3 days of sustainability. This could be less or significantly more depending on the distance to travel.

There is not an ideal weight. Typical weight is between 40 and 60 pounds including water and any everyday carry (EDC) items you have. This should be adjusted based upon your physical condition, preferences and length of travel. Keep in mind, that it is always easier to shed gear than to acquire needed items.

When traveling on foot or carrying a backpack, a typical person can walk 2 to 3 miles per hour on flat and solid terrain (such as a paved or dirt road) and 1 to 1.5 miles per hour on rough terrain with elevation changes or other factors.

Check your BOB twice a year to make sure everything is charged, intact, working and food is not expired. Be sure to create an inventory list of your BOB contents to keep track of items.

When building a BOB, it is easy to be overwhelmed with possible items and over-pack with non-essential items. It is always better to assemble your gear first and then find a bag to contain it all rather than finding a bag first and either not have enough space or have so much space that your are adding gear just to fill the bag.

By focusing the contents of your BOB to include items from core categories needed for survival, security and sustainability, you will ensure that you have a well-rounded and functional BOB. Each item should be carefully evaluated for its usefulness and benefit while considering weight and size. Redundant and multiple-use items are recommended. Miscellaneous or luxury items should be prioritized last.

<u>**Bug Out Bag Equipment Core Categories:**</u>

- Transportation of Supplies
- Water and Water Treatment
- Food and Food Preparation
- Clothing
- Shelter
- Fire
- First-Aid
- Light
- Hygiene
- Tools
- Communication and Navigation
- Self Defense
- Miscellaneous

Bug Out / Get Home Bag

The below list should be used for ideas and options, not as a prescriptive checklist.
This list is large and will not all fit into your BOB. Use this list as a guide of potential items that should be considered, reduced and modified to fit your personal situation and preferences.

Transportation of Supplies:

While the most obvious method of travel for a BOB is a backpack, there are other ways to transport your items. Where a backpack may be strenuous to carry, it is also the most versatile for travel over rough terrain. Other methods of carrying items may be less physically demanding on flat and even terrain but limit your ability to travel off roads or over obstacles.

☐ Backpack, internal or external frame with hip belt
☐ Rolling duffel bag (Eagle Creek)

☐ Fanny pack or belt pack
☐ 4 wheeled utility cart or wagon
☐ Bike and bike trailer

Water and Water Treatment:

Water is critical to your BOB. You should always carry water and adjust the amount based on the ease of finding additional water. Be sure to have a method of treating water collected.

☐ Water
☐ Hydration bladder (Camelbak)
☐ Water bottle (Nalgene, Camelbak)
☐ Canteen - metal or plastic
☐ Collapsible water bottle (Platypus, Nalgene)
☐ Single wall stainless steel water bottle, (Klean Kanteen) - Can also double as a container for boiling water or cooking

☐ Water filter
    ☐ Straw (LifeStraw, Sawyer)
    ☐ Pump (Katadyn)
    ☐ Gravity (Platypus GravityWorks, Sawyer)
☐ Purification tablets
    ☐ Iodine (Potable Aqua)
    ☐ Sodium Chlorite (Katadyn Mircopur)
☐ Bleach
☐ Sulfate Mineral Salts (Purinize)

Food and Food Preparation:

The main choice when selecting food for your BOB is what level of preparation and cooking is required. By selecting food that is ready-to-eat and can be eaten from its original packaging, you can cut down on extra gear. Consider selecting dehydrated foods. This will cut down on food weight but will require that much more water be carried or sourced. If water is not easy to find, then dehydrated foods should be avoided.

☐ Granola bars, energy bars, oatmeal
☐ Dehydrated meals
☐ Dried fruits, nuts, trail mix
☐ Beef jerky
☐ Meal Ready to Eat (MRE)
☐ Emergency Food Ration/ Bar
☐ Hard candy
☐ Small cooking stove and fuel
    ☐ Jetboil and isobutane/propane fuel
    ☐ MSR WhipserLite, fuel bottle, white gas
    ☐ Solostove (wood burning)

☐ Alcohol stove, fuel bottle and denatured alcohol
☐ Esbit stove and solid fuel tablets
☐ Candle, 3 wick hot burning
☐ Spork
☐ Fork, knife and spoon
☐ P38 can opener
☐ Mess kit, pot, bowl and cup
☐ Metal cup
☐ Metal cook pot
☐ Pot scrubber

Clothing:

Clothing is your first-line of defense against the elements. Layering should be used to adjust to the temperature and allow flexibility.

To save space, wear shoes suitable for a bug out / get home situation as part of your everyday outfit. To cut down on the amount of clothing items, rotate the clothing in your BOB seasonally to adjust for hot or cold weather.

- ☐ Boots or sturdy hiking shoes
- ☐ Belt
- ☐ Hat / Boonie hat
- ☐ Hiking socks
- ☐ Underwear
- ☐ Pants / Shorts
- ☐ T-shirt / long sleeve shirt
- ☐ Cold weather clothing
  - ☐ Jacket or waterproof shell
  - ☐ Winter hat
  - ☐ Winter gloves
- ☐ Thermal underwear - top and bottom
- ☐ Fleece or sweater
- ☐ Balaclava or face mask
- ☐ Poncho
- ☐ Rain jacket or Gortex jacket
- ☐ Bandana
- ☐ Shemagh
- ☐ Work gloves (leather or Mechanix)
- ☐ Sunglasses
- ☐ Extra prescription glasses

Shelter:

Shelter of some form is needed to keep yourself warm and dry during inclement weather. How you choose to achieve shelter can vary widely. While a tent is a logical choice, it is not the best choice in a bug out situation due to its size and weight. A simple form of shelter is a poncho, tarp shelter or bivy bag. Depending on the climate, a sleeping bag may be needed for extra insulation. Hammocks are smaller and lighter then a tent but come with the added requirement of trees for support.

- ☐ Sleeping bag
- ☐ Sleeping pad
- ☐ Bivy bag
- ☐ Small nylon tarp (6' x 8' or 8' x 10')
- ☐ Lightweight tent
- ☐ Emergency Mylar Blanket
- ☐ Paracord
- ☐ Duct tape
- ☐ Large heavy duty trash bags
- ☐ Tent stakes
- ☐ Rain poncho
- ☐ Hammock
- ☐ Carabiners or clips

Fire:

Heat is essential for survival and fire can be used for warmth and cooking. Be sure to have multiple ways of creating fire, even in damp conditions.

- ☐ Waterproof matches (UCO)
- ☐ Lighter (Bic, Zippo)
- ☐ Butane lighter and fuel
- ☐ Ferro rod / magnesium alloy and striker (Light My Fire Swedish FireSteel)
- ☐ Solar fire starter (Solo Scientific Tinder Hot Box)
- ☐ Magnifying glass
- ☐ Tinder (WetFire, magnesium)

First-Aid:

Always pack a first aid kit. Miles of hiking, especially through rough terrain, increase your likelihood of injury. From minor blisters to major bleeding, you should be able to treat it all injuries.

- ☐ First aid kit (Level 1 or Level 1.5)

Light:

Light is essential for functioning in the dark. Be sure to have multiple sources of light and pack spare batteries.

- ☐ Flashlight, battery powered
- ☐ Extra batteries
- ☐ Flashlight, hand crank
- ☐ Headlamp
- ☐ Light sticks / glow sticks
- ☐ Candles

Hygiene:

Personal hygiene will boost morale and overall mental health. Washing your hands prevents infection and the spread of viruses and bacteria. Don't expect a daily shower but a minimal amount of hygiene is needed. Don't forget the toilet paper.

- ☐ Toothbrush and toothpaste
- ☐ Toilet paper
- ☐ Wet wipes / man wipes
- ☐ Hand sanitizer
- ☐ Sunblock
- ☐ Insect repellent
- ☐ Tampons
- ☐ Toilet paper
- ☐ Camp towel
- ☐ Soap, liquid or bar

Tools:

Tools as part of your bug out bag can be heavy and take up a lot of space. At a minimum, always have a knife. Anything beyond that should be kept as small and light as possible or excluded entirely.

- ☐ Folding knife
- ☐ Fixed-blade knife and sheath
- ☐ Multi-tool (Leatherman)
- ☐ Knife sharpener
- ☐ Folding or break-down saw
- ☐ Hatchet or machete
- ☐ Small folding shovel (entrenching tool)

Communications and Navigation:

Always pack a compass to help with navigation. Maps will further assist in plotting your course. Radios can be very useful tools for communication and information gathering but their dependence on power and potentially limited range lessens the overall benefit.

- ☐ FRS / GMRS Radio (Midland, Motorola)
- ☐ Ham Radio (Baofeng, Wouxun, Yaesu)
- ☐ AM/FM/NOAA weather radio, battery powered or hand-cranked
- ☐ Compass
- ☐ Local area maps
- ☐ Small notebook and pen (Rite in the Rain)
- ☐ Emergency whistle

Self Defense:

Personal security and self defense are important. You never know what may happen when traveling during adverse times, especially in the open.

- ☐ Handgun
- ☐ Holster
- ☐ Spare magazines
- ☐ Ammunition
- ☐ Pepper spray
- ☐ Taser
- ☐ Knife

Miscellaneous:

This section consists of additional, luxury and morale boosting items to add to your BOB as space and weight permits. There are endless possible additions. Build your bag to suit your situation, needs and preferences.

- ☐ Resealable plastic bags, various sizes
- ☐ Hand held GPS
- ☐ Portable charger battery pack (phone charging)
- ☐ Solar battery charger
- ☐ Playing cards
- ☐ Night vision goggles

- ☐ Binoculars
- ☐ Fishing gear
- ☐ Flagging tape
- ☐ Snares or snare wire
- ☐ Cash, small bills ($100)
- ☐ Dust mask (3M N100)

Testing Your Bug Out Bag:

To ensure your BOB is functional and contains items you may need, while keeping the weight manageable, you should test your bug out bag in several ways:

Take A Hike:

An easy way to assess the weight and mobility of your bug out bag is to go for a hike carrying your BOB. Start with a short distance and move to a longer distance once you are comfortable with your pack's weight and fit.

Go Camping:

Go for a weekend camping trip using only your bug out bag. This will test your ability to create shelter, make fire, cook, process water and other potential scenarios during day and nighttime conditions. Ultimately, this will allow you to assess your skills and equipment.

As an additional test, try "cold camping" which means no fire, limited or no cooking and extreme light discipline. This evaluates your ability to go undetected by others which may be necessary under some conditions.

Get Home:

To test your bug out bag in a more realistic scenario, practice your Getting Home Plan either partially or entirely on foot, carrying your BOB. This will allow you to evaluate your route, as well as resources and obstacles you make encounter along the way.

For additional difficulty, test your ability to source water from several locations along the way.

Bug Out:

As an alternate (or in addition to) carrying out your Getting Home Plan, practice your Bug Out Plan either partially or entirely on foot carrying your bug out bag.

For additional difficulty, stop and spend at least one night during your bug out exercise.

After testing your bug out bag, assess what went well and what went wrong. Make adjustments and improvements to better your plan and equipment. And be sure to resupply whatever was used.

STEP 5: Car Kit

Just like the name implies, this is a kit that should be assembled and put in each of your vehicles in the event that your car breaks down or gets stranded in a situation where help is not readily available such as during a major storm or in a remote area and you need to either get your vehicle back on the road or wait out the situation until conditions better or help arrives.

Your bug out bag should contain many of these items. If your bug out bag is in your vehicle (as it should be) then you can either remove the duplicated items from your car kit or keep them as additional or quick access items.

☐ Bug out / Get Home Bag
☐ Container to hold Car Kit contents
☐ Water, 3-day supply
☐ Non-perishable food, 3-day supply
☐ First aid kit (Level 1 or 1.5)
☐ AM/FM/NOAA weather radio, battery powered or hand-cranked
☐ Sturdy shoes and wool socks
☐ Leather work gloves
☐ Sleeping bag or wool blanket
☐ Cold weather items
   ☐ Jacket / Pants
   ☐ Hat and gloves
   ☐ Hand warmers
   ☐ Ice scraper / snow brush
☐ Extra clothing
☐ Rain gear
☐ Toilet paper, wet wipes and other toiletries
☐ Maps / GPS Unit
☐ Flashlight and spare batteries
☐ Cell phone charger
☐ Matches, lighter, butane lighter
☐ Road flare or light stick
☐ Reflective blanket or signaling material
☐ Candle
☐ Duct tape
☐ Jumper cables
☐ Jack and lug wrench
☐ Tire plug kit or fix-a-flat
☐ Tire pressure gauge

☐ Tow strap
☐ Tools:
   ☐ Folding knife
   ☐ Multi-tool pocket knife
   ☐ Small folding shovel (entrenching tool)
   ☐ Bow Saw
   ☐ Wrenches and socket set
   ☐ Adjustable wrench, pliers, vise-grip
   ☐ Screwdrivers, flathead and Phillips
   ☐ Hammer
   ☐ Pry bar / crow bar
   ☐ Bolt cutters
☐ Vehicle Fluids:
   ☐ Windshield washer fluid
   ☐ Engine oil
   ☐ Brake fluid
   ☐ Power steering and transmission fluid
   ☐ Coolant
☐ Other / Optional:
   ☐ Fire extinguisher
   ☐ Gas can
   ☐ Siphon pump / tube
   ☐ Jumper box / emergency battery charger
   ☐ 12 volt air compressor or hand pump
   ☐ Hi-Lift jack
   ☐ Come-along or winch
   ☐ Tire chains
   ☐ Ice scraper
   ☐ Compact emergency / snow shovel
   ☐ Bailing wire
   ☐ Cash, small bills ($100)

Getting Stranded in Your Vehicle:

Scenarios leading to you being stranded in your vehicle can vary widely. The most common is weather or road condition related such as snow or mud and vehicle breakdown. Other scenarios include running out of fuel or getting stuck on the road due to a major accident or road closure.

Keep your vehicle at least half full of fuel at all times to allow you to lessen the chance of running out if you get stuck, stranded, cannot easily refill or have to take a major detour to get to your destination.

Ideally, you should have enough fuel to travel 500 miles. This gives you plenty of flexibility in a disaster event to get home, bug out, or endure a fuel shortage. The typical range of a vehicle with a full tank of gas is about 400 miles.

If you become stranded, first assess the situation including; your safety, ability to get or contact help, proximity to houses or cities and your ability to either get your vehicle going again or wait for assistance.

While stranded with your vehicle, conserve battery power and fuel by not running your vehicle continuously and not using things like headlights, interior lights or the radio while the car is not running. Make sure your exhaust pipe is not blocked to prevent carbon monoxide poisoning.

Under most circumstances, you are more likely to survive if you stay with your vehicle rather than abandon it and search for help on foot.

If you must leave your vehicle, take precautions including only going a short distance away, taking supplies with you, following a road, leaving a note with information on which way you went and marking your path so you can find your way back or others can follow you.

Except in dire circumstances, do not leave in the dark.

STEP 6: 72-Hour Home Kit and Supplies

Your disaster supplies kit should contain essential food, water and supplies for at least three days. Keep this kit in a designated place and have it ready in case you need to leave your home quickly. Make sure all family members know where the kit is stored. Check your 72-hour kit twice a year to make sure everything is charged, intact, working and food is not expired. Be sure to make an inventory list of your kit's contents.

A 72-Hour Home Kit could include the following items:

☐ Containers, to hold kit contents
☐ Family First Aid Kit
☐ Water, three gallons per person or more
☐ Non-Perishable Food, three day supply:
    ☐ Ready-to-eat canned meats, fruits, vegetables
    ☐ Protein or fruit bars
    ☐ Dry cereal, granola and trail mix
    ☐ Peanut butter
    ☐ Dried fruit / nuts
    ☐ Crackers
    ☐ Canned juices
    ☐ Non-perishable pasteurized milk
    ☐ High energy foods
    ☐ Vitamins
    ☐ Comfort foods
☐ Pet food and water
☐ Mess kit with pot and pan cooking utensils
☐ Paper plates, bowls, plastic utensils and cups
☐ Paper towels
☐ Plastic resealable bags gallon and quart size
☐ Small cook stove with fuel
☐ Can opener
☐ Moist towelettes or wet wipes
☐ Toilet paper
☐ Hand sanitizer
☐ Chlorine bleach and medicine dropper
☐ Camp soap and sponge
☐ Personal Hygiene:
    ☐ Brush or comb
    ☐ Deodorant, soap and shampoo
    ☐ Tampons / feminine supplies
    ☐ Toothbrush, toothpaste and floss
    ☐ Wash cloth and camp towel
☐ Prescription medications
☐ Glasses or contact lens supplies
☐ Notebook and Pens
☐ Cell phone charger
☐ Garbage bags, large heavy duty and kitchen
☐ Plastic sheeting and duct tape
☐ Waterproof tarp, 10' x 12'
☐ Candles
☐ Flashlight or headlamp

☐ Crank flashlight
☐ Light sticks
☐ AM/FM/NOAA weather radio, battery powered or hand-cranked
☐ FRS / GMRS or Ham Radios
☐ Extra batteries in each size needed
☐ Whistle to signal for help
☐ Dust mask (3M N100)
☐ Leather work gloves
☐ Local Maps
☐ Cash, small bills ($200+)
☐ Reference Guides / Books
☐ Complete change of clothes per person, including:
    ☐ Long sleeved shirt
    ☐ Long pants
    ☐ Sturdy shoes
    ☐ Jacket
    ☐ Hat and gloves
    ☐ Rain gear
☐ Tent, lightweight
☐ Sleeping bag or warm blanket
☐ Fire extinguisher
☐ Matches, lighter, ferro rod, butane lighter
☐ Crescent wrench (to turn off utilities)
☐ Compass
☐ Multi-tool and pocket knife
☐ Fixed-blade knife
☐ For Babies and Children:
    ☐ Food / formula / bottles
    ☐ Diapers and wet wipes
    ☐ Toys, books, games, puzzles, activities
☐ Other / Optional:
    ☐ Special needs items
    ☐ Solar powered battery charger and rechargeable batteries
    ☐ 5 gallon bucket and lid
    ☐ Playing cards, games or other entertainment
    ☐ Moral boosting items and foods
    ☐ Folding shovel (entrenching tool)
    ☐ Paracord (100 ft)
    ☐ Pet items

Testing Your 72-Hour Kit:

To ensure your 72-hour kit contains all of the items you may need, you should test your kit in several ways:

Cut the Power:

Over a weekend, try turning off the power to your house from Friday night to Sunday. Then using only what you have in your 72-hour kit, spend the weekend in your house going through the tasks of cooking, eating, keeping warm or cool, monitoring information sources, contacting others and functioning day and night without electricity.

This hands-on exercise will allow you to evaluate your kit, your ability to handle the situation and any shortcoming or overlooked items.

Test Your Evacuation:

Test your ability to evacuate by assembling and loading the items from your Evacuation Checklist into your vehicle which includes your 72-hour kit. Because your 72-hour kit is likely to take up the largest amount of space, this will allow you to see if your kit will fit in your vehicle.

This will also provide an assessment of the portability and type of containers used as well as an evaluation of the location or locations of where your items are being stored.

For an added level of difficulty, set a time limit for the evacuation drill to simulate the stress of an urgent situation.

After testing your 72-hour kit, be sure to assess what went well and what went wrong. Make adjustments and improvements to better your plan and equipment. Be sure to resupply whatever was used.

STEP 7: Communications

Communication plays a valuable part in emergency preparedness both for sending and receiving information. When a crisis occurs you will want to get information about the situation as well as make contact with others to check on their safety and coordinate next actions. The most important thing is that your family have an understanding of what means of communications will be used among the group and what to do if any communication method were to fail. This is the basis of your Communications Plan.

Communications Tip:

Use a text message to communicate during or after a large scale disaster instead of making a phone call. Cell phone networks get congested and your call may not go through. Text messages use far less data and will make repeated attempts at sending.

In addition to communicating with others, it is also important to receive information on emergency situations. Below are some resources for emergency alerts and information.

Emergency Alerts and Information:

There are many sources and options for emergency alerts and information. The most common alerts being weather related events. While the availability may be different for your local area, here some sources worth understanding and investigating.

Information Media:

Traditional media outlets will be the most accessible source of emergency information and direction for most situations. These include: television, AM / FM radio, Internet news as well as social media. While these sources are readily available, the information is not always accurate. Additionally, they provide little to no advanced warnings except for weather and some natural disaster related events.

Emergency Alert System (EAS)

We are all familiar in some way with the emergency alert system. This is the robotic voice that interrupts television or radio broadcasts, usually to announce a test of the system, but sometimes to provide information on a serious event in your area. The EAS is the nation's public warning system requiring broadcasters to provide communications capability for the President to address the American public during a national emergency. The National Weather Service (NWS) activates the EAS for imminent and dangerous weather conditions. The EAS is also activated to enable state and local authorities to communicate important non-weather emergency messages such as AMBER alerts and Civil Emergency Messages.

NOAA Weather Radio All Hazards (NWR):

NWR is a nationwide network of radio stations broadcasting continuous weather information directly from the nearest National Weather Service (NWS) office. NWR broadcasts official Weather Service warnings, watches, forecasts and other hazard information 24 hours a day, 7 days a week. NWR transmitters broadcast on one of seven VHF frequencies. The broadcasts cannot be heard on a simple AM/FM radio receiver. There are many receiver options, ranging from hand-held portable units that just pick up Weather Radio broadcasts, to desktop and console models which receive Weather Radio as well as other broadcasts.

Local Government Alerts:

Many city and county agencies provide an alert system that you can sign up for. They will send texts and/or emails with information. This can include: county government, city government, police department, sheriff's department, health department, school district, department of transportation and others. If they do not have an established alert system, they may also put out important information via social media channels.

Phone Apps:

Another source of alerts and information is through phone apps. This can include: American Red Cross, FEMA, weather apps, news media apps, police scanner apps and many more.

Radio Communications:

Radio communications can be an unfamiliar topic to some, so this section contains a basic overview as well as some useful information. If your Communications Plan includes radio communication, it is crucial that everyone is aligned on the frequency and anticipated time to make contact.

Because there are an abundance of resources available for anyone seeking a more in-depth understanding of radio communications. Keeping this explanation as basic as possible, is meant to provide a general overview for anyone that is completely new to the subject.

Two Way Radios (Walkie Talkies)

These are used for short range or local communications. This is the most common and inexpensive style of radio. Two-way, walkie talkie-type radios are FRS /GMRS radios. These include common brands such as Motorola Talkabout and Midland which are typically used for recreational purposes. While there are radios that use only FRS or GMRS frequencies, many include both as well as NOAA Weather frequencies. FRS and GMRS operate on 22 channels (frequencies) and channels 23-29 are GMRS repeaters which are not typically included on recreational radios.

Transmission range increases with direct line-of-sight and can typically vary from 0.5 to 18 miles. The advertised transmission range of up to 38 miles is in ideal conditions and unrealistic for typical use.

To avoid confusion across different radio types, do not use a privacy code setting. With privacy codes on, others can hear you but you will not be able to hear them.

FRS vs. GMRS:

GMRS radios generally operate on higher power which means greater transmission range.
- FRS radios are limited to; 2 watts of power on channels 1-7 and 14-22, and 0.5 watts on channels 8-14
- GMRS radios are limited to; 5 watts on channels 1-7 and 14-22, 0.5 watts on channels 8-14, and 50 watts on channels 23-29.

GMRS requires a license to operate. FRS does not require a license
- GMRS requires a license through the FCC, good for 10 years. Cost is $70
- A single license covers you and your immediate family members

CB Radio

CB is another commonly used radio communication. CB operates on 40 channels. Channel 9 is reserved for emergency communications. In the Single Side Band (SSB) mode, which operates in the Lower Sideband (LSB) or Upper Sideband (USB), you will get greater range and less noise but can only communicate with other radios in SSB mode.

Typically, CB radios are used for short range communication, but given the right conditions, CB is capable of skipping off the ionosphere for much longer range. Typical range is 2-10 miles. With an antenna and flat terrain, this can increase to around 25 miles or more.

Ham Radio

Ham radio is a very effective and useful means of communications. It is also very complex and can be confusing to anyone that has not spent considerable time learning about the hardware, operations and rules. There are a multitude of resources on the topic for a deeper level of information than is provided here.

The main benefit of ham radio is the ability to reach a much longer distance and even over mountain ranges when using a repeater. There are also vastly more frequency options in order to avoid the crowded channels of FRS / GMRS radios.

Ham radio operation requires a license through the FCC that includes passing a test for each of the three levels of licensing: Technician, General and Amateur Extra. This license is good for 10 years and only covers the person who is licensed. Each level of license comes with rules and limitations setup by the FCC.

The Technician license allows for use above 30 MHz, in the VHF and UHF frequencies for voice communications. In broad terms, the General license allows for use in the high frequency (HF) range and the Amateur Extra license allows for use on all Amateur Radio frequencies available.

Among the most common VHF/UHF radios are the Baofeng (UV-5R, BF-F8, UV-5X3 or a variant of these). These and other common hand held radios operate on these frequency ranges:

> UHF frequency range: 400-520 MHz or narrowed to 420-450 MHz
>
> VHF frequency range: 136-174 MHz or narrowed to 144-148 MHz
>
> The Tri-Band Radios also include 1.25 meter frequencies: 219-220 MHz

Baofeng Radio - Manual Channel Programming:

1. Press the MENU key to enter the menu

2. Enter "2" "7" on the numerical keypad

3. Press MENU to select

4. Use the "up" and "down" keys to select the memory channel to enter

5. Press the MENU key to confirm

6. Press the EXIT key to exit the menu

3-2-1 Radio Plan

One common method used for emergency radio communications is the 3-2-1 plan. This is a good strategy to adopt if your detailed communications plan has not been developed or to reach people outside of your communications plan.

This plan is simple and allows you to conserve your battery power.

Just like the name implies, follow the 3-2-1 steps:

- Tune to Channel **3** (FRS/GMRS 462.6125 or CB 26.985)
- Broadcast for **2** minutes
- Do this every **1** hour, on the hour

Phonetic Alphabet

The phonetic alphabet is a way to spell out words using commonly understood codewords for each of the letters in the alphabet. It is commonly used in radio and telephone communications to avoid miscommunication.

Understanding and using the phonetic alphabet will allow for clear understanding and interpretation of communications. A table has been provided below showing the phonetic alphabet as a reference tool.

	LETTER	PHONETIC	LETTER	PHONETIC
PHONETIC ALPHABET	A	Alpha	N	November
	B	Bravo	O	Oscar
	C	Charlie	P	Papa
	D	Delta	Q	Quebec
	E	Echo	R	Romeo
	F	Foxtrot	S	Sierra
	G	Golf	T	Tango
	H	Hotel	U	Uniform
	I	India	V	Victor
	J	Juliet	W	Whiskey
	K	Kilo	X	X ray
	L	Lima	Y	Yankee
	M	Mike	Z	Zulu

FRS / GMRS, CB and Weather Radio - Channel and Frequency Charts

	CHANNEL	FREQUENCY
FRS / GMRS	1	462.5625
	2	462.5875
	3	462.6125
	4	462.6375
	5	462.6625
	6	462.6875
	7	462.7125
FRS	8	467.5625
	9	467.5875
	10	467.6125
	11	467.6375
	12	467.6625
	13	467.6875
	14	467.7125
FRS / GMRS	15	462.5500
	16	462.5750
	17	462.6000
	18	462.6250
	19	462.6500
	20	462.6750
	21	462.7000
	22	462.7250
GMRS	23	467.5500
	24	467.5750
	25	467.6000
	26	467.6250
	27	467.6500
	28	467.7000
	29	467.7250

	CHANNEL	FREQUENCY	CHANNEL	FREQUENCY
CB RADIO	1	26.965	21	27.215
	2	26.975	22	27.225
	3	26.985	23	27.255
	4	27.005	24	27.235
	5	27.015	25	27.245
	6	27.025	26	27.265
	7	27.035	27	27.275
	8	27.055	28	27.285
	9	27.065	29	27.295
	10	27.075	30	27.305
	11	27.085	31	27.315
	12	27.105	32	27.325
	13	27.115	33	27.335
	14	27.125	34	27.345
	15	27.135	35	27.355
	16	27.155	36	27.365
	17	27.165	37	27.375
	18	27.175	38	27.385
	19	27.185	39	27.395
	20	27.205	40	27.405

	CHANNEL	FREQUENCY
NOAA WEATHER	1	162.5500
	2	162.4000
	3	162.4750
	4	162.4250
	5	162.4500
	6	162.5000
	7	162.5250

STEP 8: Essential Weapons and Ammo

Firearms are a valuable tool for security. Selection of firearms and caliber is a personal choice made by evaluating your situation and choosing what best fits your needs and preferences.

As a starting point, here are some tips and information on firearms, caliber and storing ammunition.

Safety

Firearms safety is paramount, not only for yourself but for those around you. Use of a firearm should be treated with respect. All users or potential users should be trained in the safe practice, operations and care of firearms. There are lots of firearm classes available to all experience levels. Everyone in your household should be trained to a level of proficiency that is appropriate for your situation.

It is important to remember and discuss firearm safety rules before and while using a firearm.

> Firearms Safety Rules:
>
> 1. Treat every weapon as if it is loaded
>
> 2. Always keep your weapon pointed in a safe direction
>
> 3. Keep your finger off the trigger and outside of the trigger guard until ready to fire
>
> 4. Be aware of your target's foreground and background before firing

Always wear eye and ear protection while using a firearm. A good alternative to traditional ear protection is electronic sound amplification headsets or earplugs that allow you to hear sounds and conversation clearly while protecting your hearing. There are also non-battery powered options such as Decibullz earplugs with percussive filters. Suppressors are also effective at reducing sound although the cost may be prohibitive.

Caliber Selection

Prior to purchasing a firearm, you should evaluate and select the caliber. Ideally, you should select one handgun caliber and one rifle caliber and standardize your firearms around that caliber.

Without debating the benefits and drawbacks of each caliber, select a caliber that is; widely used and available, common to many firearms, and fits your preferences. Weight should also be a determining factor.

> **Suggested Calibers:**
> - Handgun: 9mm, .40 S&W, .45 ACP
> - Rifle: .223 (5.56 x 45), 7.62 x 39 or .308 (7.62 x 51)
> - Shotgun: 12 gauge
> - Rimfire: .22 LR

Selecting only one rifle caliber and one handgun caliber, .223 /5.56 (5.56 x 45) for your primary weapons and 9mm for your secondary weapon is a common and favorable choice.

Ammunition Compatibility

To someone new to firearms, understanding the names and specific ammunition to use in your firearm can be a bit confusing. Here is a simple breakdown.

To determine the ammunition compatible with your firearm, look on your firearm for a marking of the caliber (or gauge) that is designed for. There may be dual markings such as .223 - 5.56, which indicates that either can be used. For shotguns, there is also a shell length marking that indicates the shell lengths that can be used.

In addition to the markings on your firearm, it is important to understand various ammunition naming conventions for compatibility.

9mm:

Also called 9mm NATO, 9 x 19, 9mm Luger, 9mm Parabellum, or 9mm P

These are all essentially the same and can be used interchangeably.

.45 ACP:

Also called .45 Auto. These are the same and can be used interchangeably.

The .45 GAP round is not interchangeable with .45 ACP or .45 Auto.

.223 / 5.56:

Also called 5.56 x 45 or 5.56 NATO. Most AR-15 platforms are chambered in 5.56 or dual stamped as .223 - 5.56, which means they can use either ammunition. Rifles marked as .223 only, cannot use 5.56 ammunition.

.308:

Also called .308 Winchester, 7.62 x 51 or 7.62 NATO.

These are all essentially the same and can be used interchangeably.

.22 Rifles

Everyone should own a .22 rifle due to the fact that ammunition is extremely inexpensive and they make for a good platform to practice fundamental marksmanship. They can also be used for small game hunting and are inexpensive to purchase.

Firearm Selection

No attempt will be made to dictate what firearms you choose. Personal preference, cost, size and manufacturer quality are some of the main deciding factors. Some suggestions are provided below as general guidance:

When selecting a firearm, choose a manufacturer and model that is widely used and common to find. This allows you to easily find magazines and spare parts for your firearm as well the ability to share these items across your family or preparedness group.

Below is a list of common firearms. These are meant to provide insight, without limiting your options. There are numerous quality firearms that are not included in this list.

Common Firearms:

- Handguns: Glock 17 or 19, 1911, Springfield XD/XDM, Smith & Wesson M&P, Sig Sauer P226 or P320, H&K USP or VP9
- Rifles: AR-15, AK-47, AR-10
- Rim Fire Rifle: Ruger 10/22
- Shotgun: Remington 870 or Versa Max, Mossberg 500 or 930, Benelli M4, Beretta TX4

Handguns: Semi-Auto vs. Revolver

Select a semi-auto instead of a revolver due to ammunition capacity and speed to reload. These factors are significant enough to recommend semi-auto handguns exclusively.

Rifles: Semi-Auto vs. Bolt-Action

Select a semi-auto over bolt action for your primary rifle due to ammunition capacity, speed to fire multiple rounds and speed to reload. In addition to your primary rifle, you may choose to have a hunting or long-range rifle that is bolt-action.

Shotguns: Semi-Auto vs. Pump Action vs. Break Action

Select either a semi-auto or pump action shotgun. A break-action shotgun as part of your security and defense preps is not recommended due to the speed to reload. Extended capacity is preferred (4+ shells).

Minimum Firearms

As part of your preparedness supplies pertaining to security, the following are suggested:

- (1) Primary Rifle, semi-automatic, AR-15, .223/5.56
- (1) Handgun, semi-automatic, 9mm

Optional:

- Secondary Rifle - hunting / long-range
- Shotgun, semi-automatic or pump action,12 gauge

These quantities should be multiplied by the number of proficient firearm users within your household.

Ideally, every member of your household or group should have the same or similar firearms to share ammunition and magazines.

Minimum Ammunition

As part of your preparedness supplies pertaining to security, the following are suggested:

- Primary Rifle: 1,000 - 2,000 rounds
- Handgun: 200 - 800 rounds
- Secondary Rifle: 200 rounds
- Shotgun: 200 rounds, including 00 buck shot and slugs
- .22 LR: 2,000 rounds

Ideal Ammunition Quantities

- Primary Rifle: 3,000 - 6,000 rounds
- Handgun: 1,000 - 2,500 rounds
- Secondary Rifle: 500 - 1,500 rounds
- Shotgun: 500 round
- .22 LR: 5,000 - 10,000 rounds

These quantities should be multiplied by the number of each type of firearm you have.

Firearm and Ammunition Storage

Firearms and ammunition should be stored in a safe manner and in a secure location. Firearms should be stored unloaded with the action (bolt or slide) forward and closed. They should be kept dry and metal components should be lightly oiled to prevent rust. Ammunition should be stored in a cool, dry location, without direct sunlight.

Other Items

Here is a list of firearm related items you should have:

- ☐ (6) spare magazines for each firearm
- ☐ Gun cleaning kit and supplies
    - ☐ Bore brushes and/or bore snakes
    - ☐ Cleaning rod and patches
    - ☐ Rags, toothbrush, or cotton swabs
    - ☐ Cleaner / solvent
    - ☐ Gun oil
- ☐ Spare parts
    - ☐ Rifle
        - ☐ Bolt carrier group (bolt carrier, bolt, firing pin, etc.)
        - ☐ Spring set
    - ☐ Handgun
        - ☐ Spare barrel
        - ☐ Guide rod

STEP 9: Load-Out Gear

Load-out gear is what you would wear and carry beyond your Everyday Carry (EDC) items. This is meant to be worn and used during and after a disaster event, as the situation requires. Load-out gear centers around being prepared to engage in a fire-fight.

You should adapt, reduce and modify these lists to your specific requirements and preferences. A kit meant for home defense and close quarters battle (CQB) is much different from a kit intended for bug out on foot or long range scouting activities. Provided are some examples of manufacturers, and again, make this your own and use quality items manufactured by companies you trust. Additionally, some people like drop leg holsters and other prefer cross draw chest holsters. The choice is up to you.

No matter what you choose, make sure it fits well, is comfortable to wear for long durations, allows the ability to run and always train with your gear to make sure it is functional and familiar for when you may really need to depend on it.

Additionally, the level to which you want to blend in to a public setting should be considered and incorporated. Full load-out in camouflaged gear, a plate carrier and rifle is going to stand out in a public setting.

Level 1:

The Level 1 load-out kit consists primarily of a battle belt (either standalone or with a cobra belt placed through it). A battle belt should have padding on the inside for comfort and MOLLE on the outside to attach all of your gear. The battle belt allows for everything to be easily put on and taken off as well as having everything assembled on one item. The alternative is to belt-mount all items either clipped on to your belt or with the belt threaded through the items. This is less convenient to quickly put on and take off.

If you are not planning on using a chest rig or plate carrier it is important to also carry rifle magazines on your battle belt.

☐ Rifle
☐ Rifle sling, single point (Magpul)
☐ Handgun
☐ Battle Belt (Viking Tactics, High Speed Gear)
☐ Cobra rigger belt or similar (Viking Tactics)
☐ Handgun holster (G-Code)
☐ Handgun magazine carrier and spare magazines (2 or 3 capacity)
☐ Rifle magazine carrier, and spare magazines (1 or more capacity)
☐ First Aid Kit (Level 1 or 1.5)
☐ Tactical gloves (Oakley, Mechanix)
☐ Knife, pocket or fixed blade, in sheath
☐ Multi-tool, in sheath (Leatherman)
☐ Dump pouch or additional gear pouch
☐ Flashlight (or part of Level 2), in pouch
☐ Radio (or part of Level 2), in pouch

Level 2:

The Level 2 includes everything from Level 1 and adds a chest rig or plate carrier to increase the number of magazines carried as well as some additional gear if desired. Even though a chest rig and plate carrier serve the same basic purpose, carrying plate armor is a large step up in your safety which is worth the extra cost and weight.

- ☐ Level 1 items and:
- ☐ Chest Rig or Plate Carrier
- ☐ 3 to 8 rifle magazines
- ☐ 0 to 3 handgun magazines
- ☐ Flashlight, in pouch
- ☐ Knife (if not part of Level 1), in sheath
- ☐ Radio (if not part of Level 1), in pouch
- ☐ Additional gear pouches

Level 3:

Level 3 includes everything from Levels 1 and 2 but adds provisions to get you through a day (or more if necessary). This includes a day pack and means of hydration. This kits contains similar items as your bug out bag but is meant to be lighter and sustain you for a shorter duration.

- ☐ Level 2 items and:
- ☐ Day pack
- ☐ Hydration pack or hydration bladder inside your day pack
- ☐ Water
- ☐ Food, 1 day supply or more
- ☐ Fire making items
- ☐ Rain poncho or waterproof jacket
- ☐ Spare clothes and extra socks
- ☐ Wet wipes / man wipes
- ☐ Insect repellent
- ☐ Sunscreen
- ☐ Paracord
- ☐ Water purification or filter
- ☐ Stove, fuel and mess kit (optional)
- ☐ Ammunition (optional)

Levels of Body Armor:

Here is a quick rundown on body armor type and capabilities. Do your research and purchase what fits your needs and budget. Remember, any body armor is better than no body armor. If financially feasible, avoid steel plate armor due to the weight. You will feel every extra pound after extended wear.

Soft Body Armor - Good for stopping handgun rounds. Lightweight, thin and concealable.

- Level IIA
  - Lowest level of protection from some handgun rounds and shotgun buckshot. No rifle ammunition protection.
- Level II
  - Will stop most common handgun rounds and shotgun buckshot. No rifle ammunition protection.
- Level IIIA
  - Most common soft armor. Will stop nearly all handgun rounds and 12 gauge slugs. No rifle ammunition protection.
- Level IIIA+
  - Will protect against nearly all handgun rounds and protection from sharp objects. No rifle ammunition protection.

Hard Body Armor - Good for stopping handgun and rifle rounds. Larger and heavier, not concealable.

- Level III
  - Capable protecting against up to 7.62 rifle rounds
- Level III+
  - Capable protecting against up to 7.62 rifle rounds and light armor piercing rounds such as 5.56 x 45
- Level IV
  - Capable protecting against up to .30 caliber armor piercing rifle rounds

STEP 10: Tools and Equipment

Beyond what is included in your bug out bag and 72 hour kit, tools and equipment are a valuable addition to your preparedness supplies. What separates these supplies from all the others, is that these items are non-essential. This means that if you need to evacuate or bug out, all of these items could be left behind with no impact to your immediate survival. The list is just a portion of potential items that could be useful.

For a bug-in or shelter-in-place scenario, all of these items would help make functioning easier. These are not meant for long-term situations but they will provide benefit as long as your energy and fuel supplies last.

- ☐ Protective Equipment
  - ☐ Heavy leather gloves
  - ☐ Safety glasses
  - ☐ Ear protection
  - ☐ Dust Mask
- ☐ Cooking
  - ☐ Propane grill
  - ☐ Camp stove
  - ☐ Pots and Pans
  - ☐ Kitchen utensils
- ☐ General Tools
  - ☐ Shovel
  - ☐ Hammer
  - ☐ Wrenches and socket set
  - ☐ Adjustable wrenches, pliers, vise-grip
  - ☐ Screwdrivers
  - ☐ Gas shutoff wrench
  - ☐ Bolt cutters
  - ☐ Crow bar / pry bar
- ☐ Transporting Items
  - ☐ Wheelbarrow
  - ☐ Ratcheting tie-down straps
  - ☐ Bungee Cords
- ☐ Power Tools
  - ☐ Cordless drill and extra batteries
  - ☐ Drill bits
  - ☐ Circular saw
  - ☐ Sawzall
  - ☐ Air compressor
- ☐ Cutting Tools
  - ☐ Chain saw
    - ☐ Bar chain oil
    - ☐ 2-cycle oil
    - ☐ Extra spark plug
    - ☐ Spare chains for chain saw
  - ☐ Axe
  - ☐ Bow saw
  - ☐ Knife and axe sharpening stone

- ☐ Light
  - ☐ Lantern (gas or battery)
  - ☐ Flashlight
- ☐ Heat
  - ☐ Propane Heater (Buddy)
- ☐ Energy / Fuel
  - ☐ Gasoline
  - ☐ Propane tanks
  - ☐ Generator
  - ☐ Extension cords
  - ☐ Power strip
  - ☐ Solar powered battery charger
  - ☐ Solar panels
- ☐ Sanitation
  - ☐ Five gallon bucket
  - ☐ Toilet seat lid
  - ☐ Cat litter
  - ☐ Garbage bags
  - ☐ Hand soap and dish washing soap
  - ☐ Tub and washboard
  - ☐ Portable wash bag (laundry)
  - ☐ Hand sanitizer and bleach
  - ☐ Disinfectant (Lysol, Clorox)
  - ☐ Clothesline or rack
  - ☐ Laundry soap (camp soap)
  - ☐ Paper towels and hand towels
  - ☐ Toilet paper
- ☐ Shelter
  - ☐ Tent
  - ☐ Tent repair kit
  - ☐ Hammer
  - ☐ Duct tape
  - ☐ Tarp
- ☐ Entertainment
  - ☐ Board games
  - ☐ Playing cards
  - ☐ Activity books
  - ☐ Fiction / non-fiction books

Reference Guides and Books

General Preparedness:

- *LDS Preparedness Manual Handbook 2: Provident Living*
- *Dare to Prepare!* by Holly Drennan Deyo
- *Handbook to Practical Disaster Preparedness For The Family* by Arthur T Bradley, Ph.D.
- *Emergency Preparedness: A Practical Guide For Preparing Your Family* by Evan Gabrielsen
- *How to Survive The End of The World as We Know It: Tactics, Techniques, and Technologies for Uncertain Times* by James Wesley Rawles
- *The Survival Group Handbook: How to Plan, Organize, and Lead People For a Short or Long Tern Survival Situation* by Charley Hogwood

Medical and First Aid:

- *The Survival Medicine Handbook: A Guide For When Help Is Not on The Way* by Joseph Alton, M.D. and Amy Alton, A.R.N.P.
- *Alton's Antibiotics and Infectious Diseases: The Layman's Guide to Available Antibacterials in Austere Settings* by Joseph Alton, M.D. and Amy Alton, A.R.N.P.
- *Where There Is No Doctor* by David Werner, Carol Thuman and Jane Maxwell
- *Where There Is No Dentist* by Murray Dickson
- *Family Medical Guide* by American Medical Association

Security and Defense:

- *Holding Your Ground: Preparing For Defense If It All Falls Apart* by Joe Nobody
- *Without Rule of Law: Advanced Skills to Help You Survive* by Joe Nobody
- *Prepper's Home Defense: Security Strategies to Protect Your Family by Any Means Necessary* by Jim Cobb

Food Storage:

- *Emergency Food Storage and Survival Handbook: Everything You Need to Know to Keep Your Family Safe in a Crisis* by Peggy Layton
- *Food Storage: For Self-Sufficiency and Survival* by Angela Paskett
- *The Emergency Pantry Handbook: How to Prepare Your Family For Just About Everything* by Kate Rowinski

Bug Out Bags:

- *Build the Perfect Bug Out Bag: Your 72-Hour Disaster Survival Kit* by Creek Stewart
- *Realistic Bug Out Bag, 2nd Edition: Prepare to Survive* by Max Cooper

Survival Skills:

- *SAS Survival Handbook, Third Edition: The Ultimate Guide to Surviving Anywhere* by John 'Lofty' Wiseman